Fun Fan Facts:

The Unofficial NBA Edition

Orlando Magic

Everything Young Magic Fans Should Know

By: Jake Liam

Dedication

For everyone who has ever visited Orlando and thought, "I could live here." And for the Magic fans who already do - you picked a great team.

THE NBA BY THE NUMBERS

MOST NBA CHAMPIONSHIPS*

- CELTICS (18) [trophies] [†]
- LAKERS (17) [trophies]
- WARRIORS (7) [trophies]
- BULLS (6) [trophies]
- SPURS (5) [trophies]

As of the 2024-25 Season. † One Trophy = 4 Championships.

NBA HISTORY SNAPSHOT

- **1946** NBA Founded
- **1954** Shot Clock Introduced
- **1979** 3-Point Line Added
- **2023** NBA Cup Introduced

BIG NUMBERS

$156 million
Stephen Curry's est. earnings in the 24-25 season

7'7"
Tallest player in NBA history (Gheorghe Mureşan & Manute Bol)

30 | 4 | 82

- **30** Teams Competing in the NBA
- **4** Playoff Rounds
- **82** Games Per Season

ORLANDO MAGIC
IN THE NBA

- FOUNDED: 1989 [†]
- NBA TITLES: 0
- CONFERENCE TITLES: 2*

20 Playoff Appearances

*† Founding dates are complicated & may cause arguments at Thanksgiving. Ask someone born before color TV. All Titles reflect pre-relocation franchise history. * As of 2024-25 Season.*

NBA ALL-TIME MVP LEADERS

KAREEM ABDUL-JABBAR (6) ★ MICHAEL JORDAN (5) ★ BILL RUSSELL (5)

EASTERN CONFERENCE

- Atlantic – **Celtics**
- Atlantic – **Nets**
- Atlantic – **Knicks**
- Atlantic – **76ers**
- Atlantic – **Raptors**
- Central – **Bulls**
- Central – **Cavaliers**
- Central – **Pistons**
- Central – **Pacers**
- Central – **Bucks**
- Southeast – **Hawks**
- Southeast – **Hornets**
- Southeast – **Heat**
- Southeast – **Magic**
- Southeast – **Wizards**

WESTERN CONFERENCE

- Pacific – **Lakers**
- Pacific – **Clippers**
- Pacific – **Warriors**
- Pacific – **Suns**
- Pacific – **Kings**
- Northwest – **Nuggets**
- Northwest – **Timberwolves**
- Northwest – **Thunder**
- Northwest – **Trail Blazers**
- Northwest – **Jazz**
- Southwest – **Mavericks**
- Southwest – **Rockets**
- Southwest – **Spurs**
- Southwest – **Pelicans**
- Southwest – **Grizzlies**

Introduction

Welcome, fans! Whether you're new to cheering for the Orlando Magic or you've been bleeding the team colors your whole life, this book is packed with fun, exciting facts about your favorite team. Get ready to impress your friends and family with everything you know about the Magic.

Quick Timeout

This book is packed with stats. Like, A LOT of stats. Every fact was checked, double-checked, and triple-checked. But here's the thing about basketball history: not everyone agrees on everything. Ask someone who watched games before color TV and someone who grew up with instant replay and you'll get two completely different answers. My dad, stepdad, uncle, and grandpa all argued about the same fact. Four people. Four answers. All of them think they're right. So if you spot something that doesn't match what you've heard, congratulations. You might be a bigger fan than the people who helped make this book. And honestly? That's pretty cool.

HOW IT WORKS

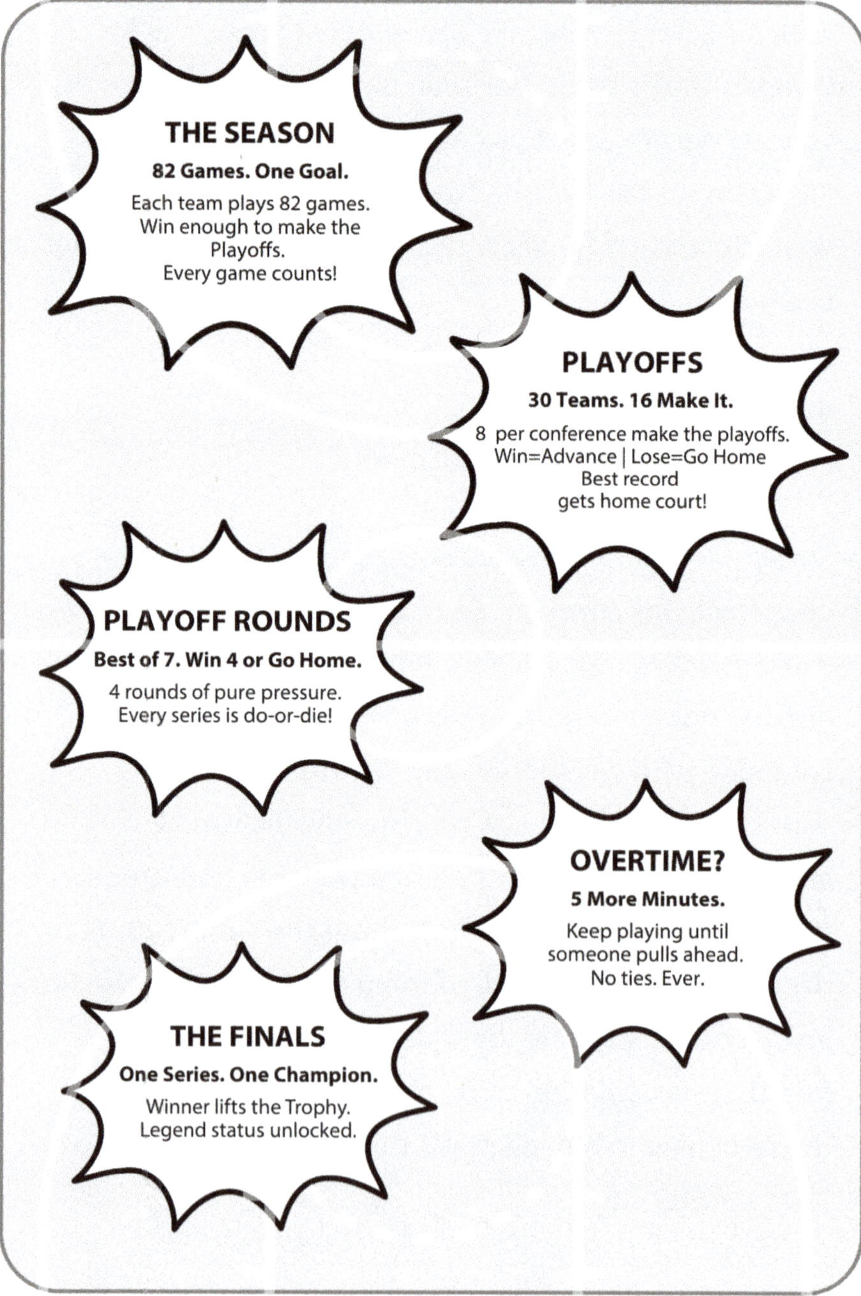

THE SEASON
82 Games. One Goal.
Each team plays 82 games.
Win enough to make the
Playoffs.
Every game counts!
PLAYOFFS
30 Teams. 16 Make It.
8 per conference make the playoffs.
Win=Advance | Lose=Go Home
Best record
gets home court!
PLAYOFF ROUNDS
Best of 7. Win 4 or Go Home.
4 rounds of pure pressure.
Every series is do-or-die!
OVERTIME?
5 More Minutes.
Keep playing until
someone pulls ahead.
No ties. Ever.
THE FINALS
One Series. One Champion.
Winner lifts the Trophy.
Legend status unlocked.

How the NBA Works

At first glance, basketball feels simple. Ten players. One ball. Two hoops. Go.

Then the NBA adds the layers.

An 82-game regular season. A draft where bad teams pick first. Playoffs that last two full months. Superstars who can change everything with one trade. Dynasties that rise, fall, and rise again.

And somehow, it all works.

The NBA is built on one big idea: every team gets a chance to reset, reload, and rise again. No relegation. No dropping down to a lower league. Just basketball, every night, from October through June.

It is a league designed for drama, stars, and comebacks. And once you understand the flow, it is impossible to stop watching.

The League Setup

The NBA has 30 teams, spread across the United States and Canada. Those teams are split into two conferences:

- Eastern Conference
- Western Conference

Each conference has three divisions, mostly based on geography. Divisions matter for scheduling, but not as much as they used to.

Every team plays 82 regular season games, usually from October through April. Home games. Road games. Back-to-back nights. Long road trips. The season is a marathon before the sprint even starts.

Win games, and you climb the standings. Lose too many, and the pressure builds fast.

How Games Are Played

An NBA game has four quarters, each lasting 12 minutes. That means 48 minutes of game time, plus timeouts, free throws, and the occasional coach argument that adds another 20 minutes nobody planned for.

Scoring is simple:

- A shot inside the three-point line is worth 2 points
- A shot beyond the arc is worth 3 points
- Free throws are worth 1 point

If the score is tied at the end of regulation, the game goes to overtime, which lasts 5 minutes. Still tied? Another overtime. Keep going until someone wins.

There is a shot clock too. Teams have 24 seconds to take a shot. No standing around. No holding the ball forever. Keep it moving.

The Regular Season Race

The regular season is long for a reason. It tests everything.

Depth. Health. Focus. Patience.

Teams play opponents from both conferences, but they face conference rivals more often. By the end of the season, each conference's top teams have earned their playoff spots the hard way.

The goal is simple: make the playoffs. But there is a twist.

The NBA Cup

In 2023, the NBA added something new to the middle of the season. Something with actual stakes. They called it the In-Season Tournament, now known as the NBA Cup.

It works like this: Every team plays a small group stage during November and December, with special court designs that look like nothing else in basketball. The best teams advance to a knockout round held in Las Vegas.

The winners split a prize pool. Players earn bonus money. And for the first time, a team could lift a trophy before the playoffs even started.

Some fans are still warming up to it. Some players love it. But the moment a team starts treating it seriously and a crowd shows up buzzing in December, it feels like something.

Which, honestly, sounds about right.

The Play-In Tournament

Instead of sending the top eight teams from each conference straight to the playoffs, the NBA added something new. The Play-In Tournament.

Here is how it works:

- Teams ranked 1 through 6 in each conference are safe
- Teams ranked 7 through 10 fight for the final two playoff spots

The 7 and 8 seeds have an advantage. Win once and you are in. Lose and you still get one more shot. The 9 and 10 seeds have to win twice in a row just to earn a first-round matchup.

It turns the end of the season into a sprint. Every game suddenly matters more. Fans love it. Coaches age rapidly.

The NBA Playoffs

Once the playoffs begin, everything tightens.

Sixteen teams enter. Eight from each conference. Every round is a best-of-seven games series. That means the first team to win four games moves on:

- First Round
- Conference Semifinals
- Conference Finals
- NBA Finals

Home-court advantage matters. Crowds get louder. Rotations get shorter. Superstars play heavier minutes. One bad quarter can flip a series. One great performance can define a career.

By the time the NBA Finals arrive in June, only two teams are left. One from the East. One from the West. Four wins away from a championship. Four wins away from history.

The NBA Draft: Hope Begins Here

Here is where the NBA gets clever. Every summer, new players enter the league through the NBA Draft. Teams take turns selecting college players, international stars, and teenagers straight out of high school.

The teams that finished with the worst records get the best odds to pick early through the Draft Lottery. It is not guaranteed, but it gives struggling franchises a real shot at changing their future with one pick.

That means one bad season does not doom you forever. It might actually change everything. Some franchises are rebuilt by a single draft night moment.

Hope shows up wearing a new jersey.

No Relegation. All Pressure.

Unlike many global sports leagues, NBA teams never drop down to a lower league. They always stay in the NBA.

That does not mean there is no pressure.

Fans remember losing seasons. Owners make changes. Coaches get replaced. Players get traded. Every year is a test of direction, patience, and belief.

Stars, Systems, and Showtime

The NBA is famous for its stars. But stars do not win alone.

Teams need chemistry. Coaches need systems. Role players need to deliver on the biggest stages. One injury. One hot streak. One trade deadline deal. Any of it can flip a season.

That balance between individual brilliance and team basketball is what makes the league special.

Fast breaks. Buzzer-beaters. Game 7s. And moments that get replayed forever. That is the NBA.

Once you get the flow, it is pure electricity.

Orlando Magic Facts

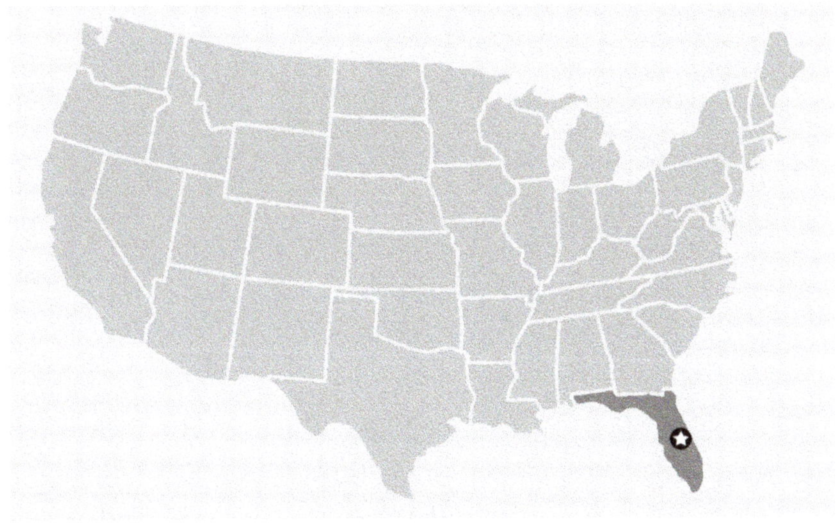

Home City

Orlando, Florida

Metro Area Population

About 2.7 Million

Home Arena

Kia Center

Arena Capacity

18,846

Conference / Division

Eastern Conference / Southeast Division

Famous Local Food

Florida orange juice, key lime pie, Cuban sandwiches, alligator bites

Chapter 1: Wishes, Wands, and a Brand New Team

1. Orlando Gets Its Wish

In 1986, a man named Pat Williams had a dream that most people thought was borderline ridiculous. He wanted to bring an NBA franchise to Orlando, Florida, a city better known for rollercoasters and sunscreen than basketball. Williams was already working in the NBA as general manager of the Philadelphia 76ers, so he knew exactly how the league worked and exactly how hard it would be to convince the owners that a theme park city deserved a spot at the table.

He campaigned relentlessly. He organized community support, secured local investors, and put together a presentation that essentially argued Orlando was a sleeping giant just waiting to wake up. The NBA was expanding in the late 1980s, adding new franchises to growing markets, and Williams made sure Orlando was impossible to ignore. The pitch worked. In April 1987, the NBA awarded Orlando one of four new expansion franchises, alongside Miami, Minnesota, and Charlotte.

The Magic played their very first regular season game in November 1989, losing to the New Jersey Nets. Not exactly the storybook beginning anyone had scripted. But nobody builds a great story without a rough first chapter, and Orlando was just getting started.

2. What's in a Name?

Before there was a roster, before there was a coach, before there was even a practice gym, the new Orlando franchise needed a name. So the organization did something genuinely fun: they asked the fans. More than 4,000 name suggestions poured in from across central Florida, which is a lot of opinions for a team that had never played a single game.

Some of the suggestions were perfectly reasonable. "Heat" was on the list, though Miami ended up claiming that one. "Juice" made the cut, which would have made for a very interesting jersey. "Fire" was popular. "Tropics" had some support. In the end, the selection committee landed on "Magic," and it fit the city in a way none of the other names quite could. Orlando was already home to Walt Disney World and a half-dozen other theme parks built entirely around the idea of wonder and imagination. Magic was not just a name. It was a personality.

The color scheme leaned into it too, with a blue, black, and silver palette that felt a little electric, a little mysterious. The whole identity said: something special happens here. Whether the basketball would live up to that promise was another question entirely.

3. Nick Anderson: The First Magic Man

Imagine being the very first draft pick in a brand new franchise's history. No pressure at all. Just you, your jersey, and the weight of an entire city's basketball future sitting squarely on your shoulders. That was the situation Nick Anderson walked into when Orlando selected him 11th overall in the 1989 NBA Draft out of the University of Illinois.

Anderson did not just become the first pick. He scored the first points in Magic history, the first basket, the very first moment of what would become decades of Orlando basketball. He stayed with the team for ten full seasons, one of the longest tenures in Magic franchise history, and he was genuinely good, a long, athletic wing who could defend and create his own shot. During the Shaq-and-Penny era of the early 1990s, Anderson was the steady third piece who made the whole machine run more smoothly.

He is also, unfortunately, remembered for one of the most painful moments in franchise history, but that story belongs in Chapter 3. For now, appreciate Nick Anderson as the guy who showed up first and stayed the longest. Every great franchise has one of those players. He was Orlando's.

4. The Luckiest Ping-Pong Ball in History

The 1991-92 Orlando Magic finished with a record of 21 wins and 61 losses. That is a difficult season by any measure. But losing that many games turned out to be the best thing that ever happened to the franchise, because it put their ping-pong ball in the NBA Draft Lottery alongside all the other teams who had also struggled, and on lottery night, Orlando's ball was the one that came up first.

That ping-pong ball was worth a seven-foot center out of Louisiana State University named Shaquille O'Neal, and he was about to change everything. The Magic had one of the worst records in the league that season, which gave them the best odds in the lottery, and for once the math worked out exactly the way it was supposed to. Some NBA franchises wait decades for a moment like that. Orlando waited three years.

Shaq arrived in Orlando in the fall of 1992 as a 20-year-old who had already been on the cover of Sports Illustrated twice before playing a single professional game. The city had no idea what was coming. Actually, the whole league had no idea what was coming.

5. Building a Home

The Magic played their first decade of basketball at the Orlando Arena, a 15,000-seat facility in downtown Orlando that opened the same year the team did. It did the job. It hosted the roaring crowds of the Shaq-and-Penny era and saw the franchise rise from expansion laughingstock to Eastern Conference champion in the span of six seasons. For a building that was never really designed to become legendary, it accumulated a lot of memories.

By the late 1990s the arena had been renamed Amway Arena after a naming rights deal, and by the mid-2000s it was already being discussed as too small and too outdated for a franchise with championship aspirations. The replacement, Amway Center, opened in 2010 as one of the most technologically advanced arenas in the NBA at the time, sitting right in the heart of downtown

Orlando with a design that felt unmistakably modern. It seated over 18,000 fans and immediately became one of the better home court advantages in the league.

In 2023, the arena was renamed the Kia Center after a new sponsorship agreement. The building is the same. The energy inside it, on the right night with the right team on the floor, is exactly what Pat Williams probably pictured back in 1986 when everyone told him his dream was ridiculous.

6. Shaquille O'Neal: The Diesel (1992-1996)

There is no way to fully explain what Shaquille O'Neal looked like to opposing defenses in the fall of 1992 without sounding like you are exaggerating, so just know that everything that follows is completely accurate. He was seven feet one inch tall, weighed around 300 pounds, and moved with the kind of speed that made scouts question whether they were measuring him correctly. He was 20 years old. He had never played an NBA game. And he was already the most physically dominant player anyone in the league had ever seen.

His rookie season was not a quiet adjustment period. He averaged over 23 points and nearly 14 rebounds per game, won Rookie of the Year, made the All-Star team, and put the entire league on notice that something genuinely new had arrived. The problem for opposing teams was not just his size. It was that he was also fast, also skilled, and also playing with a level of enthusiasm that made every game feel like a personal mission. Centers who tried to guard him one-on-one often ended up being carried off the floor, not literally, but close enough.

Shaq spent four seasons in Orlando before leaving for the Los Angeles Lakers as a free agent in 1996, and Magic fans have had complicated feelings about July 18th, 1996, ever since. He gave the franchise its first taste of real greatness. The fact that he left before delivering a championship is the one asterisk on an otherwise extraordinary chapter in Orlando history.

7. Anfernee Hardaway: Penny (1993-1999)

The story of how Penny Hardaway ended up in Orlando is one of the better trade stories in NBA history. The Magic had won the draft lottery for the second year in a row and held the first overall pick. Golden State had the third pick and desperately wanted Chris Webber. Orlando wanted Penny Hardaway. So they made a deal.

On draft night, Orlando selected Webber with the first pick. Golden State selected Hardaway with the third. Then they swapped. Golden State sent Hardaway plus three future first-round picks to Orlando in exchange for Webber. The Magic got the player they wanted AND extra draft capital. Golden State got one season of Webber before he forced his way out of town. They have spent the decades since quietly not bringing this up.

Hardaway was a six-foot-seven point guard at a time when the league had never really seen a six-foot-seven point guard, which meant he had no natural defensive matchup and could see over the top of virtually every defense in the NBA. Paired with Shaq, he formed one of the most dangerous one-two combinations in basketball, a pairing so gifted that Nike built an entire sneaker line around it called "Lil' Penny," featuring a wise-cracking puppet that somehow became more famous than some actual NBA players.

The injuries came eventually, as they so often do, and Penny never quite reached the ceiling everyone had mapped out for him. But from 1993 to 1996, he and Shaq were must-watch television, and every Magic fan who was old enough to see it in real time will tell you exactly where they were sitting.

8. Tracy McGrady: T-Mac (2000-2004)

A 6-foot-8 wing from Florida who could score from anywhere named Tracy McGrady came to Orlando in the summer of 2000. He was 21-year-old and had spent three seasons in Toronto quietly suggesting that he might be one of the best players on the planet. The Magic gave him the chance to prove it, and he responded by becoming the most unstoppable offensive player in the NBA for two full seasons. In 2002-03, he led the league in scoring with over 32 points per game. The following year he led the league again. Back-to-back scoring titles, both times with a team that was not built to compete for a championship, which made the numbers even more remarkable.

The frustrating part of the T-Mac era in Orlando is that the talent was never properly surrounded. He was carrying the offensive load almost entirely by himself, putting up numbers that the stat sheets could barely contain, while the roster around him cycled through players who were solid but not quite at his level. The Magic made the playoffs once in his four seasons and lost in the first round. Great player, difficult situation, no championships.

McGrady was traded to the Houston Rockets in 2004 in a deal that brought Steve Francis to Orlando. It was the kind of trade that made complete sense on paper and felt completely wrong in person, the way certain things in sports always do. Orlando has had several of those moments. T-Mac's departure is near the top of the list.

9. Dwight Howard: Superman (2004-2012)

The Orlando Magic selected Dwight Howard with the first overall pick in the 2004 NBA Draft, and the scouting report at the time basically said: enormous, athletic, raw, enormous. He was 18 years old, had skipped college entirely, and arrived in the NBA looking less like a rookie and more like something a special effects team had built for a superhero film. Which, as it turned out, was exactly the right comparison.

Howard became the best defensive center in basketball within a few seasons, winning three consecutive Defensive Player of the Year awards from 2009 to 2011. He led the Magic back to the NBA Finals in 2009, their first trip since the Shaq-and-Penny era, and turned the Amway Center into one of the most intimidating home courts in the Eastern Conference. The Superman nickname came naturally, embraced so fully that

Howard once appeared in the Slam Dunk Contest wearing an actual cape, which is covered in more detail in Chapter 3 because it absolutely deserves its own section.

The Howard era ended messily, with a trade demand and eventually a deal to the Lakers in 2012 that left Orlando fans with the same complicated feelings they had carried since 1996. The Magic have a particular talent for developing generational players and then watching them leave. The consolation is that they clearly also have a talent for developing generational players in the first place.

10. Paolo Banchero: The Don (2022-present)

Paolo Banchero was the first overall pick in the 2022 NBA Draft, and if that sentence sounds familiar, it is because Orlando has a genuine gift for landing the top selection when it matters most. Banchero arrived from Duke as a six-foot-ten forward with the ball-handling of a guard, the strength of a power forward, and a competitive personality that showed up clearly in his very first NBA games. He was not easing in. He was not adjusting. He was immediately playing like someone who had been waiting his whole life for the moment to start.

He won Rookie of the Year in 2022-23, averaging over 20 points per game and doing it with a composure that made experienced defenders look slightly confused. The numbers were impressive. The way he got those numbers was more impressive. Banchero consistently finds ways to create his own shot against good defenders, which is the skill that separates good players from players who become franchise cornerstones.

The comparison that Magic fans are allowing themselves to make quietly, in careful voices, is the Shaq-and-Penny parallel with Banchero and Franz Wagner forming the new version of that blueprint. It is early. The pressure is enormous. Based on everything Banchero has shown so far, the pressure does not appear to be bothering him at all.

11. From Nobody to the Finals (1994-95)

In 1994-95, the Orlando Magic won 57 games in their sixth season of existence. To put that in perspective, most NBA franchises spend their first six years learning how to lose with dignity. Orlando skipped that part entirely and went straight to making the entire Eastern Conference deeply uncomfortable.

The team that showed up for the playoffs that spring was built around a 23-year-old center who bench-pressed small buildings for fun and a 22-year-old point guard who saw the entire floor like he was watching from the ceiling. They were flanked by Horace Grant, who had just won a championship with the Chicago Bulls and arrived in Orlando with the specific energy of someone who had already done this before and was perfectly happy to do it again. The Magic were young, fast, loud, and completely unbothered by the idea of being taken seriously.

Then came the second round. The Chicago Bulls. Michael Jordan had just returned late in the season after his first retirement, leaving Scottie Pippen to carry the defending champions, and Chicago was still legitimately dangerous. Orlando beat them in six games anyway, which sent the city into a level of celebration that was frankly disproportionate for a conference semifinal and absolutely completely proportionate for a conference semifinal. They were going to the Eastern Conference Finals. A team that had lost 61 games just three years earlier was two wins away from the NBA Finals. Pat Williams, somewhere, was doing the longest "I told you so" in Florida history.

12. Four Free Throws. Four Misses. One Broken Heart.

This is the one. Every franchise has one. The moment that lives permanently in the back of the fan's brain, surfacing at inconvenient times, like during quiet dinners or right before sleep. For Magic fans, it is four free throws. Specifically, four free throws that Nick Anderson attempted late in Game 1 of the 1995 NBA Finals against the Houston Rockets, and four free throws that Nick Anderson did not make.

The setup was almost too perfect. Orlando was up by one point with seconds remaining. Anderson got fouled. All he needed was one made free throw to put the game essentially out of reach. He missed the first one. Fine, that happens. He missed the second one. Less fine. Houston tied the game, forced overtime, and took control from there. Suddenly the Magic were down by one with the ball and a chance to win. Anderson got fouled again. Two more free throws. He missed them both. Houston won in overtime.

Imagine watching that in person. Imagine being Nick Anderson. He shot under 50 percent from the free throw line for the rest of his career, a number that tells you everything about what those four misses did to his confidence. He never talked about it as something he moved past. He talked about it as something he learned to carry. Houston went on to win the series four games to zero, sweeping a team that had beaten Jordan's Bulls a month earlier, and the 1994-95 Magic went from "dynasty in the making" to "what could have been" in the span of one overtime game. The ping-pong ball giveth. The free throw line taketh away.

13. Superman Has Entered the Building

On February 16th, 2008, Dwight Howard strapped on a genuine Superman cape over his Orlando Magic jersey, accepted a basketball from a child dressed as Lois Lane because why not, and then dunked the basketball so emphatically that the Slam Dunk Contest crowd made a noise that you can still find on YouTube and watch repeatedly during moments when you need to remember that sports can be genuinely joyful.

The dunk itself was not technically the most difficult in the contest. Howard was six-foot-eleven and could simply reach up and deposit the ball through the rim without fully jumping if he felt like it. The genius was the theater. The cape. The character. The complete commitment to a bit that most professional athletes would have quietly talked themselves out of at some point between the idea stage and the actual performance stage. Howard did not talk himself out of anything. He leaned in until the bit became a defining moment of his public identity and an image that an entire generation of basketball fans carries around permanently.

He won the contest, obviously. The cape is currently displayed in the Naismith Memorial Basketball Hall of

Fame, which means that somewhere in Springfield, Massachusetts, there is a Superman cape in a glass case next to actual championship trophies and MVP awards, and that is genuinely one of the best things about the NBA as an institution.

14. Back to the Finals (2009)

Fourteen years after Nick Anderson's free throws, the Orlando Magic returned to the NBA Finals. The 2008-09 team was built around Dwight Howard's defensive dominance and a collection of shooters so accurate that opposing coaches spent the entire Eastern Conference Playoffs looking at their offensive schemes and then looking at Orlando's defensive coverage and then quietly putting the schemes away and staring at the ceiling.

The run was extraordinary. They beat the Philadelphia 76ers in the first round, then dismantled LeBron James and the Cleveland Cavaliers in six games in the Conference Finals, which at the time felt like one of the biggest upsets imaginable given that LeBron was in the middle of an MVP season and playing like a man on a personal mission to win a championship before anyone else got comfortable. Orlando had other ideas. Rashard

Lewis hit shots. Hedo Turkoglu hit shots. Dwight Howard made LeBron's drives to the basket feel like suggestions rather than certainties.

The Finals against the Los Angeles Lakers did not go the way Orlando hoped. Kobe Bryant and a fully operational Lakers team won in five games, and the Magic's window, it turned out, was shorter than anyone wanted. But for one spring in central Florida, the Magic reminded everyone that the 1994-95 team had not been a fluke. This franchise knew how to build something worth watching. The championship was the only part that kept slipping away.

Hedo Turkoglu brings the ball up for the Orlando Magic. Six-foot-ten with the handles of a point guard and the shot selection of someone who genuinely did not believe in bad moments. Magic fans called him Mr. Fourth Quarter. Opposing coaches called their timeouts. *Photo: Hedo Turkoglu, Orlando Magic. Photograph by Keith Allison. Licensed under CC BY-SA 2.0. Source: Wikimedia*

15. Scott Skiles and the Night Nobody Could Stop Passing

On December 30th, 1990, Orlando Magic point guard Scott Skiles handed out 30 assists in a single NBA game against the Denver Nuggets. Thirty. In one game. The record had stood at 29, set by Kevin Porter in 1978, and Skiles broke it so definitively that the NBA essentially stopped expecting anyone to challenge it. Nobody has come particularly close since. That was over three decades ago.

To understand what 30 assists actually means, consider that an average NBA team totals somewhere between 20 and 25 assists in an entire game, spread across five players and 48 minutes. Skiles matched or exceeded that number entirely by himself. Every time a teammate scored, there was a reasonable chance Skiles had something to do with it. He was the quarterback, the conductor, and the traffic controller simultaneously, running an offense that functioned like a very fast, very loud, very basketball-shaped machine.

Skiles was never a superstar. He was a stocky, tough, extremely competitive point guard from Indiana who played the game like someone who had been personally insulted by inefficiency. He later became an NBA head coach, which makes complete sense because a man who spent his playing career making everyone around him better was always going to end up teaching for a living. The record still stands. It may stand forever. And it belongs to Orlando, which is the most delightfully unexpected sentence in this entire book.

Chapter 4: Stuff, Stars, and Strange Orlando Traditions

16. Stuff the Magic Dragon

Stuff the Magic Dragon was introduced as the Orlando Magic's official mascot in 1989, and whoever was in that first meeting when someone said "what if we made the mascot a dragon named Stuff" and everyone else in the room nodded and wrote it down deserves a specific kind of credit that the sports world has never properly given them. It is a perfect decision. It makes no logical sense. It has aged magnificently.

Stuff is green. Stuff has wings. Stuff wears an Orlando Magic jersey and spends his professional life doing backflips on a trampoline, firing t-shirts into the upper deck from a cannon, and generally behaving like someone who consumed an entire theme park's worth of energy and decided basketball was the appropriate outlet. He is not subtle. He is not trying to be. He is a large green dragon at a basketball game and he has fully committed to the premise every single night for over three decades.

The name is technically a reference to stuffing a basketball, which is another way of saying dunking, which connects the mascot to the sport in a way that makes complete sense once someone explains it and zero sense before that. Children love Stuff unconditionally. Adults who attend their first Magic game and encounter Stuff for the first time go through a brief period of confusion followed immediately by acceptance. There is no middle stage. You either understand Stuff or you are about to understand Stuff.

17. The Lottery Team

The Orlando Magic have won the NBA Draft Lottery four times. Four. In a league where the lottery is specifically designed to prevent any single franchise from getting too lucky too often, Orlando has somehow walked into that room on three separate occasions and left with the first overall pick like they had the address written down in advance.

In 1992, they won the right to draft Shaquille O'Neal, who became one of the fifty greatest players in NBA history. In 1993, they won again despite having just a 1.5% chance, the longest odds to ever produce a lottery winner. They used that pick to acquire Penny Hardaway in a trade, which was a different kind of lottery win but arguably just as impactful. In 2004, they won again and selected Dwight Howard, who became a three-time Defensive Player of the Year and led them back to the Finals. In 2022, they won a fourth time and selected Paolo Banchero, who won Rookie of the Year and is currently making NBA defenders reconsider their career choices on a nightly basis.

The statistical odds of winning the lottery four times are the kind of numbers that make mathematicians briefly question their understanding of probability. Other franchises have spent fifty years trying to land a single top overall pick and come up empty. Orlando has done it four times before their franchise turned 35. There is no good explanation for this. There is only gratitude, a slight feeling of cosmic guilt on behalf of the rest of the league, and a franchise that has been handed generational talent at a rate that should probably be studied by someone with a PhD.

18. Disney World and the Magic

When the NBA shut down completely in March 2020 due to the pandemic and needed somewhere to restart the season in a controlled bubble environment, the league looked at its options and chose Orlando's ESPN Wide World of Sports Complex, a facility literally inside Walt Disney World. Which means the NBA Finals, one of the most watched sporting events in America, was decided inside a theme park. The trophy was awarded approximately two miles from Space Mountain. This is a completely real thing that happened.

For the Magic specifically, the bubble was a complicated experience. They were eliminated in the first round by the Milwaukee Bucks while playing home games inside a theme park resort with no fans in attendance, surrounded by Disney infrastructure, which is not exactly the playoff atmosphere the franchise had envisioned. But the broader point stands: Orlando's relationship with the entertainment industry is so deep that when the entire sports world needed somewhere magical to hide for six months, they called the city that literally named its basketball team after the concept of magic.

Walt Disney World opened in 1971. The Magic were founded in 1989. The two institutions have coexisted in central Florida for the entirety of the franchise's existence, and while the Magic have occasionally struggled to compete with a theme park that has rides, characters, and fifty years of global brand recognition, they have also given Orlando something Disney never could: a reason to care deeply about a sport played by real people having real moments that nobody scripted in advance.

19. The Starting Five of Weird Facts

Every franchise accumulates strange facts the way a dryer accumulates socks, and Orlando is no exception. Consider the following, presented without ranking because they are all equally wonderful.

The Magic once had a player named Bo Outlaw, which is genuinely one of the best names in NBA history and deserves to be acknowledged. Outlaw played for Orlando in the late 1990s and early 2000s and was a defensive specialist known for energy, effort, and a name that sounded like it belonged to a character in a western film. The NBA has had many great names. Bo Outlaw is a top ten finalist in any serious discussion.

Orlando is also one of the few franchises in NBA history to have drafted a player who was simultaneously pursuing a professional baseball career. Shaquille O'Neal, in addition to everything else he was doing, recorded a rap album during his time in Orlando that actually went platinum. Penny Hardaway had a puppet with a more active social life than most people. The 1994-95 team featured a player named Tree Rollins, whose nickname was "Tree," because he was seven feet tall, and nobody felt the need to explain further. The Magic's first ever head coach was Matty Guokas, whose name is a genuine test of confidence to pronounce aloud in public. These are the facts that do not fit neatly anywhere else but absolutely needed to be included.

20. Game Night at the Kia Center

There is a specific kind of energy inside the Kia Center on a night when the Magic are playing well and the crowd is locked in, and it is difficult to describe to someone who has never experienced it without sounding like you are overselling it, so instead here are some specific details and you can form your own conclusions.

The building holds just over 18,000 people and sits in the middle of downtown Orlando, surrounded by restaurants and bars that fill up two hours before tip-off with people in blue jerseys having conversations that are entirely too intense for something that has not happened yet. The game presentation inside is loud in a way that feels deliberate rather than accidental, with music and lighting timed to the action on the floor. When Dwight Howard was in his prime, opposing teams genuinely dreaded playing in Orlando because the atmosphere made their free throws feel harder. Psychological home court advantage is real, and the Magic have historically been good at manufacturing it.

The tradition of fans waving white towels during big moments goes back to the early 1990s, which means there are adults in Orlando who grew up watching their parents wave towels at basketball games and now wave towels themselves while their own children look at them with the specific expression children reserve for moments when their parents are being extremely embarrassing in the best possible way. That is a legacy. That is a franchise doing something right.

21. Franz Wagner: The Other Half of Everything

Franz Wagner was drafted 8th overall by the Orlando Magic in 2021, which means Orlando selected him a full year before they selected Paolo Banchero first overall in 2022, which means the Magic essentially built their future core backwards and it worked out perfectly anyway. This is completely on brand for a franchise that wins lotteries it has no business winning and trades third picks for first picks and generally operates by its own internal logic that somehow keeps producing correct answers.

Wagner is from Berlin, Germany, which makes him one of the more internationally traveled players in a league that has genuinely become a global sport. He played college basketball at the University of Michigan, where he was excellent, and then arrived in the NBA and was immediately better than expected, which is a pattern he has continued every single season since. He averaged over 22 points per game in 2023-24, doing it with a combination of footwork, court vision, and a competitive instinct that makes him infuriating to guard because he does not have one primary move. He has seventeen primary moves and will use whichever one you left open approximately one second ago.

The thing that makes Wagner genuinely exciting to watch is not any single skill. It is the combination of all of them working simultaneously, the way a well-built engine is impressive not because of any individual part but because everything fits together and runs cleanly. Orlando fans have watched enough individual brilliance leave through the exit door to genuinely appreciate what it looks like when a player commits to the city. Franz Wagner has committed to the city. The city has noticed.

22. The Brothers Wagner

Moritz Wagner, Franz's older brother, also plays in the NBA, currently alongside Franz in Orlando, which means the Magic have two brothers from Berlin on their roster simultaneously, which would be a heartwarming story in any context but is especially heartwarming in a city that has historically watched its best players pack their bags and head somewhere else.

Moritz is a center, three years older than Franz, who has carved out a solid NBA career through the specific combination of skill, effort, and a willingness to do whatever the team needs that coaches love and stat sheets sometimes undersell. He is not the star of the story. He knows he is not the star of the story. He appears to be completely fine with this, which is either genuine contentment or the performance of a lifetime, and either way it is impressive.

The image of two brothers from the same family playing on the same NBA team in the same city is the kind of thing that gets made into a documentary eventually. Their parents fly from Germany to watch games with a frequency that suggests they have worked out a very good deal on transatlantic flights. Franz and Moritz grew up playing basketball together in Berlin, dreaming about the NBA the way kids from Berlin dream about the NBA, which is with slightly more geographical improbability than kids from, say, Indiana. They both made it. They both made it to the same team. If Stuff the Magic Dragon could cry, he absolutely would during the pregame introductions.

23. The Rebuild Done Right

Between 2018 and 2022, the Orlando Magic were not good. This is stated plainly and without judgment, because rebuilding in the NBA is a legitimate strategy that requires patience, organizational clarity, and the ability to watch a lot of losses without losing faith in the direction. The Magic lost a lot of games during those years. They finished last in the Southeast Division multiple times. They were the kind of team that appeared on other teams' schedules as a circled date for a reason that was not flattering.

What they were doing, quietly and methodically, was accumulating draft picks, developing young players, and building a roster philosophy around the idea that sustainable success requires real talent rather than patchwork solutions. It is the kind of approach that is easy to describe and genuinely difficult to execute, because every losing season requires an organizational belief that the losing is temporary and the building is real. A lot of franchises announce rebuilds and then panic halfway through and make trades that feel good in October and terrible by February. Orlando did not panic.

By 2023-24 the Magic had one of the youngest rosters in the league, one of the best young players in the league, and a playoff berth that felt less like a surprise and more like the first payment on a very long investment. The process was painful. The results are starting to arrive. The fans who sat through the losing years are beginning to look like people who held a stock nobody believed in right up until the moment everyone believed in it.

24. The Kia Center: A Building Worth Talking About

The Kia Center opened in 2010 and was immediately considered one of the finest arenas in the NBA, which is the kind of compliment that sounds modest until you realize there are thirty NBA arenas and being considered one of the finest means something specific. The building was designed with a downtown Orlando sensibility, glass and steel and angles that catch the Florida light in a way that looks genuinely dramatic on television and even more dramatic in person.

The technology inside the arena has been updated consistently since opening, because the one thing a modern sports facility cannot afford is to feel dated, and ownership has invested in the building the way ownership should invest in buildings that represent the public face of a franchise. The scoreboard is enormous. The sound system is the kind of thing that makes you feel the bass in your chest during player introductions, which is either thrilling or medically inadvisable depending on your perspective and your cardiologist's opinion.

The name changed from Amway Center to Kia Center in 2023, which prompted the usual mild fan complaints about corporate naming rights that accompany every arena rename in every sport in every city, lasting approximately two weeks before everyone just started calling it the Kia Center and moved on with their lives. The building is the same. The hot dogs are the same. The experience of watching Paolo Banchero post up a slower defender and score over him with an elegance that seems unfair for someone his size is very much the same. A name is just a name. What happens inside is what matters.

25. Why the Best Is Still Coming

Here is where the Orlando Magic stand right now, stated as clearly and honestly as possible: they have two of the best young players in the NBA, a coaching staff that knows how to develop talent, an ownership group that has demonstrated patience during the hard years and commitment during the building years, and a fanbase that has been through enough heartbreak to appreciate what it looks like when something real is being constructed.

Paolo Banchero is 22 years old. Franz Wagner is 23. Moritz Wagner is 26. The core of this team has not yet reached the age at which most NBA players enter their prime. The championships that Orlando has chased since 1989 have not arrived yet, but the foundation being built right now is more deliberately constructed than anything the franchise has assembled since the Shaq-and-Penny era, and it is being built with the specific knowledge of what went wrong those other times.

The Magic have given their fans a lottery win, two Finals appearances, a Superman cape in the Hall of Fame, a dragon mascot who fires t-shirts from a cannon, and thirty years of moments that range from devastating to transcendent and back again. They have also given their fans something rarer than any of that: a genuine reason to believe the next chapter is the best one. The ping-pong balls have been kind. The talent has been real. The building is happening in front of your eyes. Pay attention. This one is going to be worth watching.

Bonus Trivia Quiz!

You think you are a true Magic fan? Try this bonus quiz!

1. Who was the very first draft pick in Orlando Magic history?

A) Shaquille O'Neal
B) Penny Hardaway
C) Nick Anderson
D) Scott Skiles

2. What was the name of the man who campaigned to bring an NBA franchise to Orlando in the late 1980s?

A) Pat Riley
B) Pat Williams
C) Pat Ewing
D) Pat Sajak

3. How many name suggestions did fans submit when Orlando was choosing its team name?

A) 400
B) 4,000
C) 40,000
D) Just one, and it was "Magic"

4. Which team did Orlando beat in the 1995 Eastern Conference Semifinals on their way to the NBA Finals?

A) New York Knicks

B) Indiana Pacers

C) Chicago Bulls

D) Cleveland Cavaliers

5. How many free throws did Nick Anderson miss in the closing seconds of Game 1 of the 1995 NBA Finals?

A) 1

B) 2

C) 3

D) 4

6. What was the name of Penny Hardaway's famous puppet from the Nike commercials?

A) Big Penny

B) Lil' Penny

C) Mini Penny

D) Penny Jr.

7. Which team did Orlando trade with to turn the third overall pick into the first overall pick in the 1993 NBA Draft?

A) Los Angeles Lakers

B) Chicago Bulls

C) Golden State Warriors

D) Phoenix Suns

8. How many consecutive Defensive Player of the Year awards did Dwight Howard win?

A) 1

B) 2

C) 3

D) 4

9. What costume element did Dwight Howard famously wear during the 2008 Slam Dunk Contest?

A) A Batman mask

B) A Superman cape

C) An Iron Man helmet

D) A Spider-Man suit

10. How many assists did Scott Skiles record in a single game on December 30th, 1990, setting an NBA record that still stands?

A) 25

B) 27

C) 29

D) 30

11. Where was Franz Wagner born?

A) Munich, Germany

B) Hamburg, Germany

C) Berlin, Germany

D) Frankfurt, Germany

12. How many times have the Orlando Magic won the NBA Draft Lottery?

A) 1

B) 2

C) 3

D) 4

13. What is the name of the Orlando Magic's official mascot?

A) Blaze the Dragon
B) Stuff the Magic Dragon
C) Spike the Magic Dragon
D) Dunk the Dragon

14. In which season did Tracy McGrady win his first NBA scoring title with the Magic?

A) 2000-01
B) 2001-02
C) 2002-03
D) 2003-04

15. What was the Orlando Magic's arena renamed in 2023?

A) Amway Center
B) Disney Sports Arena
C) Kia Center
D) Magic Kingdom Arena

Super Fan Secret Challenge

Only a true Magic fan will know this.

(No Answer Provided)

The Orlando Magic have retired several jersey numbers in honor of their greatest players. One of those retired numbers belonged to a player who was never actually on the Orlando Magic roster. He was honored because of his enormous impact on the city and the franchise during a specific period in team history, despite the fact that he played his championship seasons somewhere else entirely. Which jersey number did the Orlando Magic retire for a player who never won a championship while wearing Magic blue?

Answer Key

1. C) Nick Anderson

2. B) Pat Williams

3. B) 4,000

4. C) Chicago Bulls

5. D) 4

6. B) Lil' Penny

7. C) Golden State Warriors

8. C) 3

9. B) A Superman cape

10. D) 30

11. C) Berlin, Germany

12. D) 4

13. B) Stuff the Magic Dragon

14. C) 2002-03

15. C) Kia Center

NBA PLAYOFF BRACKET

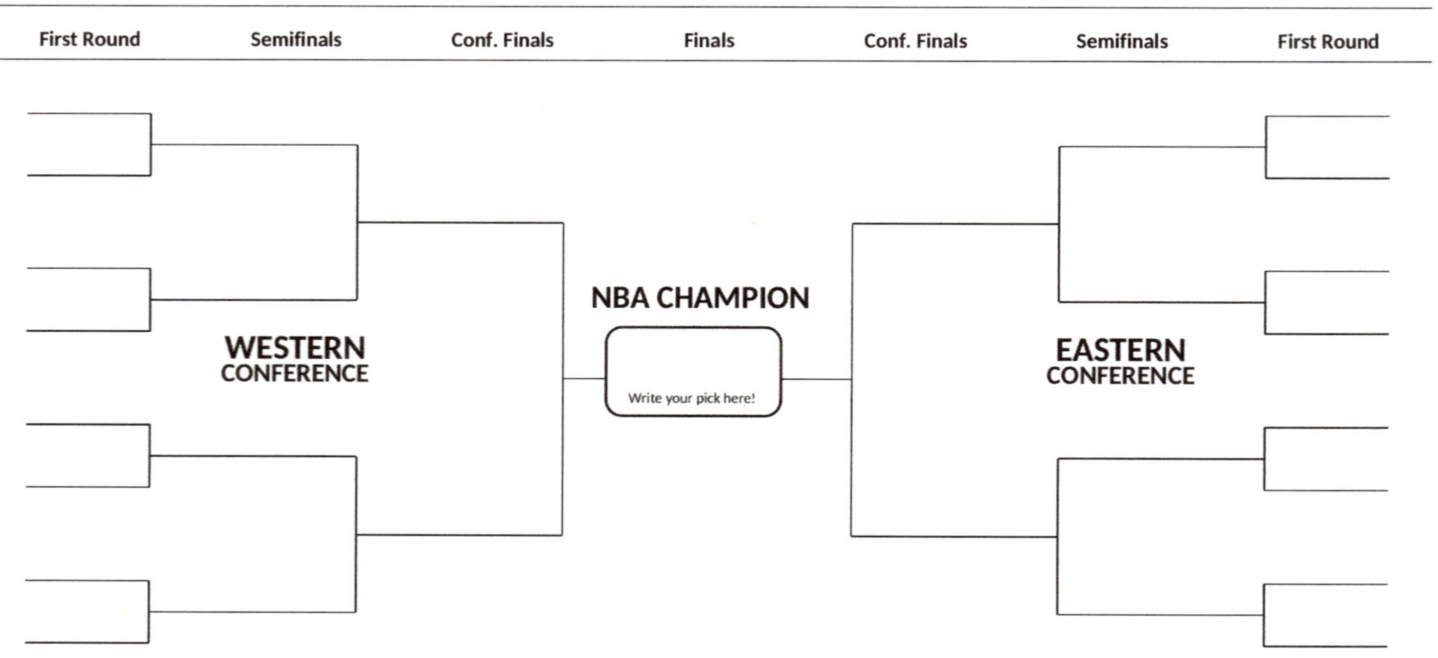

* Fill in your picks and try not to argue with your friends about it!

Part of the Fun Fan Facts: The Unofficial Sports Guide Series

Be the Boss of the Playoffs

You've broken down the matchups. You know which superstar takes over in the fourth quarter. You've seen the bench units that quietly decide series. You've watched the adjustments coaches make when their backs are against the wall.

Now it's time to stop watching and start deciding.

On this page, you are not just a fan. You are the Head Coach drawing up the last play with three seconds left on the clock. You are the GM who built this roster. You are the analyst who saw it all coming.

This is not just filling out a bracket.

This is building your championship run.

Sixteen teams enter the NBA Playoffs. The path is brutal. Best of seven. No shortcuts. No hiding. Every round gets louder, harder, and more personal.

This bracket is your Playoff Control Room.

The Game Plan

1. Survive Round One: Start with the opening round. Which matchup is going seven games? Who has the closer? Who folds under pressure? Make the calls.

2. Feel the Momentum: As you move into the Conference Semifinals and Conference Finals, things change. Role players become heroes. Stars feel the weight. Trust your reads.

3. Own the Finals: Trace your picks all the way to the NBA Finals. When the confetti falls and the trophy is raised, you'll find out who earned it.

House Rules: Circle your boldest upset. That is your official "I knew it" moment.

Choose Your Weapon: Pencil if you want flexibility. Pen if you trust your instincts. Sharpie if you believe in chaos.

Because once the playoffs tip off, there is no rewinding Game 7.

Make your picks. Trust your basketball brain. And let the playoff drama begin.

Fun Facts Wrap-Up

You made it through! You're officially a true superfan! Now it's time to put your knowledge to the test. Share these facts with friends and see who really knows their team best.

Love the series?

Your reviews help other fans discover Fun Fan Facts. If you enjoyed this book, we'd really appreciate you sharing your thoughts and leaving a review.

Want more Fun Fan Facts?

Scan the QR code below to visit our site and explore bonus trivia, challenges, and special extras - including new teams, future series, and collectible fun as they're released.

Collect All the Fun Fan Facts Series!

Check off every book you read. See the full set on Amazon. Search "Fun Fan Facts Jake Liam."

World Cup 2026 Edition

☐ Algeria	☐ Scotland	☐ Morocco
☐ France	☐ Brazil	☐ Switzerland
☐ Paraguay	☐ Ivory Coast	☐ Curaçao
☐ Argentina	☐ Senegal	☐ Netherlands
☐ Germany	☐ Canada	☐ Tunisia
☐ Portugal	☐ Japan	☐ Ecuador
☐ Australia	☐ South Africa	☐ New Zealand
☐ Ghana	☐ Cape Verde	☐ United States
☐ Qatar	☐ Jordan	☐ Egypt
☐ Austria	☐ South Korea	☐ Norway
☐ Haiti	☐ Colombia	☐ Uruguay
☐ Saudi Arabia	☐ Mexico	☐ England
☐ Belgium	☐ Spain	☐ Panama
☐ Iran	☐ Croatia	☐ Uzbekistan

World Cup 2026 Group Edition

☐ Group A	☐ Group F	☐ Group K
☐ Group E	☐ Group J	☐ Group D
☐ Group I	☐ Group C	☐ Group H
☐ Group B	☐ Group G	☐ Group L

English Football Edition

☐ Arsenal F.C.

☐ Aston Villa F.C.

☐ Chelsea F.C.

☐ Everton F.C.

☐ Fulham F.C.

☐ Liverpool F.C.

☐ Manchester City

☐ Manchester United

☐ Newcastle United F.C.

☐ Tottenham Hotspur

☐ West Ham United

☐ Wrexham A.F.C.

NBA Edition

☐ Atlanta Hawks

☐ Boston Celtics

☐ Brooklyn Nets

☐ Charlotte Hornets

☐ Chicago Bulls

☐ Cleveland Cavaliers

☐ Dallas Mavericks

☐ Denver Nuggets

☐ Detroit Pistons

☐ Golden State Warriors

☐ Houston Rockets

☐ Indiana Pacers

☐ LA Clippers

☐ Los Angeles Lakers

☐ Memphis Grizzlies

☐ Miami Heat

☐ Milwaukee Bucks

☐ Minnesota Timberwolves

☐ New Orleans Pelicans

☐ New York Knicks

☐ Oklahoma City Thunder

☐ Orlando Magic

☐ Philadelphia 76ers

☐ Phoenix Suns

☐ Portland Trail Blazers

☐ Sacramento Kings

☐ San Antonio Spurs

☐ Toronto Raptors

☐ Utah Jazz

☐ Washington Wizards

About the Author

Jake is a 13-year-old sports fan who loves football, American football, and basketball. He plays soccer as a goalie and dreams of one day playing for West Ham United and helping teach kids to love the game. His passion for sports runs in the family - his dad was a professional baseball player, and his stepdad sparked his love for West Ham. Through the Fun Fan Facts series, he shares the fun and excitement of sports with fans everywhere.

www.ingramcontent.com/pod-product-compliance
Lightning Source LLC
Chambersburg PA
CBHW050043040726
47599CB00015B/1778